For Lady K

Follow God's directions
& you'll never lose!

If She Only Knew...

If She Only Knew...

"OPENING YOUR EYES"
TO THE TRUTH ABOUT MEN

*A journey through the mind of a man, the keys to
a successful relationship and a better you*

Ronny Myles

Library of Congress Control Number:		2012907684
ISBN:	Hardcover	978-1-4771-0443-9
	Softcover	978-1-4771-0442-2
	Ebook	978-1-4771-0444-6

This book was printed in the United States of America.

To order additional copies of this book, contact:
Xlibris Corporation
1-888-795-4274
www.Xlibris.com
Orders@Xlibris.com
115869

TABLE OF CONTENTS

If She Only Knew...

Opening Your Eyes To The Truth About Men

will explain many mysteries and myths about relationships and dating. Through this journey into the mind of a man, you'll discover things about him that either you didn't know or were misinformed about regarding how to get to his heart.

This book is designed to not only give women valuable insight on men, but also explain why women end up in situations they never dreamed of or swore they would never be in. Along with identifying the problems in relationships, remedies, practical applications and simple solutions are only a page away!

While learning about what makes a man tick, the lights will come on about yourself, the decisions you've made, and what part you played in the demise of your own relationships. The good news is that it can be turned around, but it starts with you making a decision and being brave enough to change your thinking.

Most books tell you how to handle situations *after* things happen, but this book teaches you how to "reverse the curse" and prevent disaster *before* it ever occurs!

Prepare your mind for a fascinating journey and a life-changing experience that will have an impact on you and the way you've thought about relationships in the past because things are about to change for the better!

REMAIN "THE HUNTED"

After being in a relationship for a while with a man, women oftentimes wonder why their man seems to develop eyes for other women or why they have a problem keeping the interest of their own man. Well, let's examine the psychology of a man. A man is a hunter by nature and he will operate on that principle without giving it a second thought or doing it on purpose. Men are designed to seek out and conquer; that is a critical character trait for men to have because it moves life forward and accomplishes things that are necessary for the evolution of all mankind.

The biggest mistake that a woman can make is to stop being hunted! As soon as you become fully accessible, predictable, or captured, the hunt is over, and the hunter is off to conquer the next challenge that for the moment is out of his grasp. Ladies, a hunter will not chase, pursue, or go after anything that isn't moving or running away, hence the phrase "the thrill is in the chase."

Men are designed to work first, then reap the benefit of that work. Men have to feel as though they have accomplished something as a direct result of the work that they put in. **If a man doesn't have to work to get you, he won't work to keep you!**

A man's nature is to seek out, design a plan to attack, conquer, glory in his accomplishment, rest, and start the process all over again because that is the core of all male behavior. Women are designed to nurture, cultivate, incubate, and take care of what she has to make sure it lasts.

That's the fundamental difference between a man and a woman; men capture things and bring it home, but that's as far as he usually goes; in his eyes, his work is complete. The woman, on the other hand, cares for what was brought home and put under her supervision. She's not as concerned about going out and capturing something as a man would be; her fancy is tickled by maintaining what was captured. What floats the man's boat is the fact that he saw something that was a challenge, but he was finally able to conquer it!

Hunting makes a man sharpen his skills, challenges his intellect, and strokes his pride if he ultimately wins or gets the prize! Ladies, this is why, at first, the man is relentless in getting you to date him or give up the goods. He will say or do anything to get what he wants, just as a hunter will set whatever trap necessary to capture his prey. The chase is when his passion is burning at its peak, so all his energy goes into his "pursuit of happiness." Have you ever noticed that when you finally give in to his advances, his interest in you seems to head for the hills, and if he is interested after the first time, it seems like he only wants that one thing?

Well well well, here is the reason why! You literally *have nothing else to offer*! When a man finally gets the goods, his conquest is done, and even if he gets it only one time, that's usually enough! His mission to break down your defenses is complete—you gave it up. Now he needs to reignite his flame by taking on another conquest or mission that will give him a challenge, while you, on the other hand, he already knows how to disarm, and you are no longer something to pursue. So he no longer works to get you; he goes straight for the thing that you surrendered—your body and your sex.

LIPSTICK ON A PIG

By now, you've heard the phrase of "putting lipstick on a pig." The whole meaning behind that statement is this: whatever the nature or essence of something or someone is, **that is what it is**—no matter how you dress it up! Women have the beauty of trying to see the best in everything and everyone deep inside of them; that's part of who they are by nature, and that is necessary for them to be mothers, wives, homemakers, and caretakers of the family. The downside to that character trait is that women often allow it to override realities, especially in relationships.

Men are very simple creatures and easy to figure out. What makes it difficult for a woman to figure out a man is because **she sees him as she thinks he *could be***, not as he is! The writing is always on the wall and the signs are there, but they are overlooked due to a number of things. Here are some of the main reasons women let their guard down before they should, and they pay for it every time!

- You need a male figure for your children.
- You're so desperate to be married.
- Your friends have a man.
- What's wrong with me?
- Why am I still single?
- You need financial assistance.
- He's so sweet.
- He's so fine.
- He's cute.
- You're horny.

Men are very patient if there is something that they either want real bad or if they see a great deal of value in it. Since that is the case, *you* have to be and remain of value to him. Women are so worried about him going somewhere else if she doesn't give it up that they will sacrifice any standards that they have, trying to keep a man around or to get a man!

If he can't wait, then that's not who you want or need anyway! Men are masters at recognizing weaknesses and exploiting them; that's what makes us crafty hunters and gamers. Competition is what we live for and losing is not an option we entertain.

A man may be sweet, fine, tall, handsome, sexy, and everything else you could dream about the perfect man being, but in the end, a man is a man. Just as there are many cars, some with more features than others, but the bottom line is that they all have the same basic features: wheels, windows, seats, doors, etc. At the end of the day, it's a car! So it goes for a man—some are cuter than the next, but a man's essence doesn't change. That was given to him by God to make a man, a man. Therefore, as the saying goes, "you can put lipstick on a pig, but it's still a pig!"

THE GRASS IS GREENER

There is a very good reason why the saying "The grass is greener (or seems greener) on the other side of the fence" came about. The desire for something is always stronger when you don't have it in your possession. I bet you aren't as excited about your car or house as you once were before you got them, right? Our appetite decreases after acquiring what we've longed for, and as time goes on, we all have to find ways to remember the beauty in what we do have and spend time making it precious and increase in value. Psychology and perception are two very powerful *P*s.

The reason a man may think the grass is greener on the other side is because when he is standing in his own yard, which is his relationship with you, all he can see are the areas that are fading and need to be fertilized or watered. The places that need attention in his own yard represent the work that he has to do, so he may stay away from doing it. However bad it looks, it's not as appealing because it reminds him of the fact that he has neglected his own yard.

Looking at the neighbor's yard, which represents another woman, the grass appears to be greener because he hasn't been in that yard yet. Every yard has its spots, but it takes someone to treat it right in order for it to remain beautiful!

A WORD TO THE MEN!

Here is a wise suggestion for the fellas: stay home and take care of your own yard! Your yard will grow weeds and look neglected if you spend all of your time away from home. Have you ever seen how a yard looks when the owner is gone too much or on vacation? Everyone that passes by your place will know you are either gone or neglecting it, and before you know it, the landscaper is knocking at your door!

If a man is taking care of his own yard, everyone that passes by will admire it and wonder how he manages to keep it so beautiful! Consider this, men: when a landscaper is looking for a yard to put his finishing touches on and expand his business, he's going to be looking for the yard that has been neglected—in which case, *your* woman may just consider making an appointment to be treated right and beautified by the landscaper!

An unsatisfied woman can't help but show it, and no matter what she does to hide it, when pressed, she will let it out. Men can't blame their ladies for finding ways to express how they feel, whether it be to a man or another woman. Make sure you as a man are doing what you need to in order to make sure she is confident in being your only lady, and watch the change in her countenance.

**A woman's countenance reflects the contentment
of her relationship with her man.**

LESSONS FROM NATURE

One of the easiest ways to figure life out is to examine nature and the way the animal kingdom works. It is truly amazing how male animals are similar to the human males and female animals are similar to human females. Take lions for instance; the males are almost identical in behavior to a man. They are considered to be the "king of the jungle," but in reality, there are other animals that even a lion wouldn't mess with.

Male lions spend most of their time chillin', lying around, waiting for dinner to be brought to them, don't spend as much time with the kids as the mom, let the females get the dinner; once the dinner is caught, he shows up and inserts his position as the "king" as though he's done something to help, goes out to solicit more females to be part of his pride, has multiple female lionesses but won't let another male get anywhere close to them, makes the most noise but does the least amount of work around the house, and the list goes on. Don't get me wrong, I know all men aren't like the lion, but it's funny how close they are in their behavior.

Now ladies are a trip too! Women look for the big, strong, attractive male in the group and then start flaunting their feminine attributes to get his attention. They prance around, bat their eyes, cross their legs, give deep eye contact, flash those pearly teeth and do a whole lot of things to get noticed. All of these things may work, *but* when a woman surrenders too quickly and becomes captured, she has played her trump card and doesn't have much leverage left!

That's the biggest *no-no* in the book. You have to use what you have to attract; then you've got to play your game right! Even if you desperately want that man, you can't let him know how much, he needs to stay in pursuit of you. You have to make him want you and it doesn't matter how you look—you have to work with what you have to the best of your ability. The gift of attracting or enticing a man was given to all women, but you must learn how to use it to keep him around also.

No hunter—be it man or animal—wants prey that they didn't have to work to get. A cheetah can chase down a gazelle or a rabbit in a flash, however, if the prey is caught too quickly or stops running, the predator won't eat it right away. Oftentimes, the cheetah will encourage the prey to get up and keep running because its hunting thirst hasn't been satisfied yet! There is an aggression that must be satisfied and fulfilled in order for the predator to feel like they have accomplished something because that boosts their ego.

Something inside of the male species requires that we chase and pursue to feel worthy of the catch! In other words, if you keep a man feeling like he has to work to get close to you, you'll keep his hunting skills sharp and that will keep his interest. You have to be predictable and unpredictable at the same time—predictable that you will work your female persuasiveness to open his nose up and leave him wanting more, but unpredictable of what reward he will receive.

RENT TO OWN

Rent to own, rent to own, rent to own . . . whether ladies care to admit it or just don't realize it, when it comes to relationships, ladies are renting themselves out all the time! Think of yourself as a house, your boyfriend or man as a potential buyer, and the purchase of a home as a marriage. Buying a home is a huge responsibility that takes a tremendous amount of commitment, so a lot of thought has to go into it before making a purchase of that magnitude.

This somewhat explains the reason why most men seem to be reluctant to get married. Most men have a one-track mind and aren't designed to multitask as you ladies are, so the thought of all of the responsibilities of owning a home (a marriage) can be overwhelming. He has to continually maintain the yard, the garage, the driveway, the gutters, the paint, the landscaping, the mortgage note, the insurance, the taxes, the interior, the HOA dues, etc. (You get the picture.)

The dream of owning a home makes most people sacrifice, save, and start getting their credit and other affairs in order to make that dream a reality. In other words, it takes work and commitment, but when it comes to relationships, here's where it gets interesting. When a woman surrenders herself or makes it easy for a man to win her affection, she is renting herself out!

Picture this, rented property (cars, apartments, equipment, etc.) is usually mistreated and dogged out because multiple people have been there, used it up so they have low regard for it. Since they didn't have to work or sacrifice to get it, they have no long-term plans for it. The same goes for a woman that puts herself in that position. A man realizes when a woman hasn't kept herself or has a habit of surrendering herself and he will treat her just like rented property.

It's a temporary place or thing for them, and they know that going in, so they have no level of commitment or allegiance to it. Women often say to themselves, "Why do I keep attracting the wrong type of men?" *Stop renting yourself out*! Renting attracts the riffraff! Consider yourself worthy of the purchase (marriage) and the sacrifice a man must make to have you!

Now that brand-new home is a woman that has taken the time to know her worth and it/she is not for rent, but for *purchase only*! If a buyer (a man) can't afford the house, the home doesn't drop in value just to have someone live there. The right buyer with the right credentials will eventually come along and deserve that home because they made whatever sacrifice it took to get it! When he finally gets the keys and moves into that house, he will appreciate it, love and respect it, make others respect it, and do whatever it takes to maintain it! Have you ever gone to a friend's house that just got new carpet? Oh, you're taking those shoes off because this is a precious investment that they had to wait for, make changes for, save up for, and sacrifice for! If a man has to work to get something, he will work to keep it because anything worth having is worth working for!

Ask yourself this question, ladies: are you that beautiful house that is increasing in value and makes every man look at it like "*Wow*! I sure would love to take up residency in there. That's my dream house!" Or are you a run-down apartment that has had multiple occupants and anyone can rent as long as they have a deposit and their credit and credentials don't matter? **Let's face it—every man is not fit to own a home, ladies!** Some deserve to be in an apartment, and only *you* can determine who moves in to your house. You get exactly what you allow yourself to have!

THE P IS *NEVER* FREE!

Casual dating? Is there really such a thing? It really depends on how you describe the term "dating." The games that men and women play are too funny these days and all too serious at the same time. A man that considers himself to be "single" or a "bachelor" usually takes the position that if he tells a woman up front that he isn't looking for anything serious or long-term but proceeds to have sex with her that, somehow, she doesn't have the right to become hooked or demand any more than that from him.

What's even more interesting is that the woman may agree to it and think that she can play by those rules without getting attached. Both parties are playing themselves and before they even know what hit them, they have both fallen into something and will soon be struggling to get out!

The problem with this way of thinking is that sex is never just "casual." Sexual intimacy is designed to bring two people together as one flesh, so when someone talks about casually having multiple partners, that is going to become an issue real quick! Why do you think that it's so hard for people to just walk away from each other even when they argue and fight all the time? That other person has a piece of their soul and they are spiritually tied to them but don't know it.

A man may be abusive to a woman but she can't seem to leave. She will often make excuses why she remains in that unhealthy relationship even though it may impact other people. Sadly, she may have children that will be subjected to this type of dysfunctional behavior. Unfortunately the children may think this is how relationships are supposed to be.

Set all the rules up front for dating that you want but when you cross that line, expect things to change! Engaging in sex with someone is the deepest exchange that you can have with another human being and that is the reason God designed sex for a marriage, not for a casual encounter. A woman's body is the most mysterious yet glorious place that a man can enter, so when she gives that part of herself away, there are going to be emotions that show up that she didn't know she had.

Her body is her personal space and it is very delicate, but because of the void that she longs to fill, she may blindly sacrifice it for the sake of feeling loved or desired. When a person is void of either self-love or they don't recognize their own value, anything that offers validation or a temporary fulfillment will usually become a quick fix for them. Ladies, please know that *good sex* may get a man, but it certainly won't keep him!

Gentlemen, please understand that you may take full advantage of trying to fill that void for her and please yourself at the same time, but you are losing a part of yourself as well. The unfortunate reality is that you really don't know what the price is until after you have jumped all in. You could end up with a woman that can't or won't let you go, diseases, unwanted children, and drama beyond your wildest dreams.

So there is a ton of truth to the title of this chapter because for everything gained, there is a price to be paid. *Everything costs something.* The *P* definitely isn't free!

HOW LONG, LORD?

"How will or how can I know if he's the one?" This question has probably been asked by every woman that has ever dated, been hurt, and is looking for a husband or new relationship. This is a legitimate question and should be asked if you are considering a courtship with a new prospect; however, most people don't exercise patience in this area.

Life has a way of manipulating us into wanting what others have (*covet*) and causing us to sacrifice what we know is right just to get that thing that we have longed for or cried out to God for. As soon as we get a visual in focus that appears to be what we desire, we allow that thing to speak into our heart/ears, which causes our emotions to start running wild, and there we go all over again.

This world is filled with the mind-set of "I want it *right now*," but there is a critical ingredient to obtaining things that we all have a tendency to miss or ignore—it's called *the process*. Everything on this earth has its own process, which is also known as *time*. Time reveals *all things*, including the answer to the question of **"Is he the right one?"**

Consider this: A woman that conceives a baby can't turn around and have the baby the next day just because she *wants* it. The process of pregnancy must run its course; then the baby can come forth. If you wanted the perfect body and desired to go from a size 14 to a size 6, you can't go to the gym and workout a few times and expect to get those results. It's a process that will only manifest over a period of time and you must remain patient and consistent while the dream manifests itself.

Knowing up front if a man is "the one" is impossible. That's like knowing how your unborn baby will look while it's still in the womb or if it will be born with a birth defect. You may be able to guess according to the ultrasound and other tests, but the truth is that you really won't know until time has passed, and the manifestation has taken place.

The same goes for determining if someone is the right person for you. You must allow the natural process and time to make the right decision but unfortunately, we jump ahead of the process and there are substantial consequences when we do that. Unwanted pregnancies, broken homes, diseases, bad or abusive relationships, multiple partners, and many more undesirable things that we all struggle with are direct results of us foregoing the process that God put into every facet of life.

You can't plant a seed today and have a tree tomorrow. You can't eat one time and be full forever. You can't snap your fingers and be on the other side of the world instantly. You can't feed a baby today and it become an adult tomorrow. You can't get on a treadmill this afternoon and be a supermodel when you get off. You can't shoot a basketball one time and go to the NBA. You can't choose to sleep with a man tonight and he turn into the perfect husband for the rest of your life!

All of these things are obtainable, but the process by which they come into their fullness requires time, patience, and commitment! When we take out the waiting period or the timetable that God placed on all things to mature, we are going to pay dearly and the results will never be what we thought they would be or desired.

HURRY UP AND WAIT!

If you take a cake out of the oven too soon just because it smells good and you're hungry—you'll destroy it or it will cave in. If a baby is removed from the womb before the full term is completed—you'll have a premature baby that could have major medical issues that lasts a lifetime. Put a ten-year-old behind the wheel of a car and see what type of destruction follows. Get tired of waiting at a red light and run through it and see what happens. Keep clocking out early from work and see how long you have your job. Get yourself into the wrong relationship because you're tired of waiting or being alone and watch all hell you catch!

Every example emphasizes the importance of *waiting* and exercising patience but more importantly, the consequences of when we don't allow the process to be completed. Notice also how every scenario has the potential to affect other people's lives as well, so your haste to get what you want "right now" can cause you to make the wrong decision. Making decisions based on your emotions can bring more heartbreak for you and your loved ones than you ever imagined.

Because we have free will and consider ourselves to be grown, we go after things that our flesh tells us we need or should have, but there's a payday coming, be it good or bad. *Free will does not supersede God's timetables*!

Waiting can be the hardest thing we are called to do. When you have a vision of what you want, where you want to be, what type of person you want to marry, it can become very difficult when a shortcut or a quicker way of obtaining your dream seems tangible.

Imagine hitting the lottery but being told you have to wait two weeks to collect. You probably wouldn't get much sleep and offered a settlement for less but you could collect today, you more than likely would take that option. Hasty decisions always cause us to settle for less and the same goes for a lady that chooses to lower her standards just to have a man or a relationship.

Spend time improving yourself and preparing to be a whole person with or without a relationship so if one comes along, you're fine; if it doesn't come soon enough, you're fine! Having a man or a relationship doesn't complete or validate a woman—recognizing your own value and who God says you are is where your validation comes from.

Just as a Mercedes doesn't have to convince itself that it is valuable, a woman shouldn't have to convince herself of her worth. She only has to realize how valuable she is and be confident in knowing that she can enhance anything she touches or adds her life to. If you consider yourself to be valuable, others will too.

*Perception is reality, so be perceived as something of value and worth more than gold!

FOLLOW THE LEADER

The best way to evaluate the right man for you is really quite simple. Remove your own desires and internally read his personality résumé. What I mean by this is for you to remain at a distance (friends) long enough to let his true nature come out. When "dating," everyone plays their winning hand or comes with their 'A' game; so if that's what you base your decision to date someone on, it's only a matter of time before your dreams of a meaningful relationship crash and burn. Remember, a leopard can't change its spots, nor can a man rid himself of his fleshly nature; but just as a wild animal can be trained, so can a man learn to control that nature with God's help and instruction.

There are major questions that a woman should ask herself before getting into a relationship: "Does this man edify me and/or add to my life, or does he only want me to add something to his? Does he listen to me and is he genuinely concerned about all that happens in my world, or is he waiting for me to stop talking so he can make his desires known? Is he willing to earn the respect of my parents, or does he shy away from meeting my people? Can he have a conversation that keeps me wanting to hear him speak even more, or does his conversation usually lead to the same thing? Does he show interest in my children and their progress, or does he try to wait until they are gone or asleep to deal with me?

A man that has a genuine interest in you *must* have an interest in everything that concerns you! ***How can he care about you, but not about what you care about?*** Don't ask him if he does—*watch* him and see if he does!

If a man is really into you, he will spend time trying to earn your adoration and respect, not just your lovin'. Ladies, you have to put on your long-term glasses and be real about the signs that are right in front of you! Ask yourself this: does this man who claims to love me encourage me to be a better woman whether I'm with him or not?

Look at his character in other areas of life and see how he handles it! Is he a lackadaisical person who only has passion in the bedroom, or does he have a drive to do what's right in other areas, such as work, family and the church? No woman should have to push a man to have a relationship with God; he should be saying to you, "Baby, let's go to church" or "Let's talk about the events of the day." **You get exactly what you settle for!**

Keep your maternal instincts in check and use them for your children, not to raise or change a man! *Stop* trying to make a man into what you want him to be and wait for a man that is already what you want a man to be. **Example:** If you wanted a brand-new red car, you wouldn't go buy a black one and paint it red, would you? Look at it as if your ideal husband is that red car that has everything you ever wanted, but it had to be shipped from California to Georgia—it's coming, but you have to be patient and prepare yourself for it!

Kobe Bryant and Michael Jordan didn't have to train their NBA teammates; they prepared *themselves*, and when the *time* was right, they went into the league. The other players that were already prepared (on their own) ended up on the same team, and they were all able to enhance each other and play the game to win together! That's the way to prepare for your "game/future": Work on yourself, and God will send another prepared person who's been doing the same thing!

ARE YOU REALLY READY?

There is such a thing as the "law of attraction" that exists in the world as we know it. The main thing that a woman who is looking to attract the right man into her life must do is a self-examination. If we are all brutally honest with ourselves, we may find that we are nowhere near being prepared for the "perfect spouse" as we think. Many of us, for whatever reason, feel like we pretty much have ourselves together and we are ready for someone to enter our lives. But ask yourself these questions to see if you are really ready:

- Do you wait until God sends a man to find you?
- Do you not date and remain celibate until marriage?
- Do you let go of past hurts and transgressions against you in previous relationships?
- Do you look at all that you need to fix about you and not worry about his issues?
- Are you able to show and give love with no expectation of it being reciprocated?

Most of us are familiar with 1 Corinthians 13: 1–7, but the question is, will you operate according to these principles on a full-time basis? If you are having an issue doing any of these things or some seem harder than others, *you are **not** ready for a relationship*!

*Here is the ultimate definition of what love really means:

1 Corinthians 13:1–7

Love is patient, love is kind *and* is not jealous; love does not brag *and* is not arrogant, does not act unbecomingly; it does not seek its own, is not provoked, does not take into account a wrong *suffered,* does not rejoice in unrighteousness, but rejoices with the truth and bears all things, believes all things, hopes all things, endures all things.

*True *or* genuine love *is not an emotion or warm and fuzzy feeling; it's a continuous sacrifice of oneself that is rooted in God's Word and carried out through* discipline, *which brings change to the recipient of that* love. *Stop expecting* love *to feel good—it's a* sacrifice, *not an emotion!* Nowhere in this scripture does love express how it feels; it only says what it does and does not do. When offenses are committed against *love*, it continually gives, forgives, and tolerates *all things.* So are you really ready?

For some reason, we think the world would be a better place if *other people* would change or stop trippin'. The reality is that change starts with you and you control your own responses. We are commanded to *love* and that should be based on our obedience to God, not how someone else made us feel. Another major concern in this area of operating in *love* is that women will often withhold or not give *love* when they feel like they are being taken advantage of, taken for granted, used, mistreated, dogged out, or abused. The *love* we are supposed to give, show, and operate in is to be done *unconditionally.*

Just because you don't *feel* like doing it doesn't mean you stop performing the acts of service that God's *real love* requires. When you love the way God says to love, you are actually giving the other person the tools they need to make a change.

I'MMA MAKE YOU LOVE ME!

I'm sure the thought of "How can I make him happy or love me?" has crossed the minds of most ladies that feel like they are putting out way more than they are receiving from their partner. There is a real simple answer to this question and it may cause you to change the way you think. If you really want to know, here it is! Leave no stone unturned! In other words, study your significant other and pay close attention to everything that they need to make them feel whole. Don't just go by what they say, but by what they have a positive response to.

The key is to beat the outside world to the punch. Always be the first to provide whatever is needed and here are some examples. Every day be the first to tell him how special he is to you, how nice he looks, how good he smells, how good he makes you feel, etc. (even if he doesn't). Don't allow any other influences to say or do something you're not doing. Make your relationship airtight, where nothing else can get in because outside influences can only come in where there is a crack, a hole, or a leak.

If you make sure he is edified, satisfied, and reassured every day before he heads out into the world, not only will that seal up any openings and prevent outside influences from coming in, it will give him a confidence that his home and heart is secure with a woman that loves him and only him. Another woman's compliments and advances won't carry the same weight as yours because you got to him first and he loves you, not her. If you seduce him first, a second attempt by someone else won't work!

Ladies, you have to have that man so ready to get back home to you that he almost wants to call out and not go to work at all! It's not about the sexual side of this that will make this work, so please don't misunderstand the point here. Leave him wanting to hear what you're going to say next or what you're going to do next.

A woman has way more influence than she realizes, but it has to be used creatively to get the right results in a relationship! Think about it, how would you feel if a man did everything mentioned above to you? You want to drive a man crazy, keep him guessing and anticipating!

You want to be loved, correct? Then that's what you have to put out! You get what you give, you attract what you focus on, and you reap what you sow. So ask yourself, "Am I giving the same thing that I desire to receive?" If we allow pride and selfishness to stop us from giving someone else what they need even though we have the ability to give it, that's what will come back to us—selfishness.

If you give love with conditions and strings attached, then you will receive love with conditions and strings attached as well, which isn't true love anyway. Give what it is that you want to receive!

THE REMEDY

At this point, some of you may still be in the dark as to how to treat a man or use your feminine persuasion to get what you want and need from a man, so let me help you out. *Please get your highlighter and highlight this section* if you don't do it to any other chapter in this book! In order to make a man feel like a man or worthy of his manhood, here is what you *must do* to be successful.

- You have to make him feel useful and like you *need* his input or assistance.
- Give him assignments that require him to use his masculine physique.
- Tell him how much you appreciate what he did or attempted to do for you.
- Tell him that you'd rather have him doing it for you more than anybody else.
- If it's something he can't do, encourage him that he didn't fail, maybe next time.

Remember, ladies, men are designed to accomplish something with their own hands or by their own effort (just like in chapter 1) because that drives us and makes us feel like a man. The last place that a man wants to feel unneeded is at home or with his woman. A word to the women that have brothers and a father in their lives: If something breaks down or needs to be done that requires physical effort or some problem-solving skills, *do not call your male family members to come and do it!*

Give him the opportunity to do it first, and if he's lazy, offer to help him get it done. Even if your man can't perform the task or fix something, the biggest form of disrespect to him is to solicit the help of another male figure, family or not.

To a man, that's like him going to another woman at the job and asking her to cook his dinner or him going out to eat right before he gets home and you were there cooking! A man wants to feel as if your world depends on him (even if it doesn't), and you ladies have to be creative enough to make him *think* that it does.

Men are like a coconut—we are hard and look a little rough on the outside, but once you get to the inside, it's a totally different substance. Women have been using the wrong tools for years, and it's like they basically are trying to change a tire with a pair of pliers. Every problem has a solution, and every task can be conquered using the proper tools.

Stop trying to eat soup with a fork or cut a steak with a hammer! The proper tools used on the issue at hand yield the desired results! Encouragement is free and is the best way to get the most out of the man you already have! There is a fundamental difference between what men need and what women want: **men *need* to feel *needed*, and women *want* to feel *wanted.***

"MS. INDEPENDENT?"

The music of today has really messed up relationships rather than enhance them. All of these songs screaming "Ms. Independent" have pretty much pitted the women against the men. They give off the notion that a strong independent woman can do everything for herself and that she doesn't need a man. I agree up to a certain point; anybody can actually hold their own (man or woman) if they are financially able to support themselves and pay for everything they need to have done. That doesn't work when it comes to a meaningful relationship because money isn't everything!

If an independent-minded woman begins a relationship with a man, there is a major mind-set adjustment that needs to take place. I understand the ideology that a woman may want to maintain her sense of independence in case the relationship doesn't work out, but oftentimes, that same fight to hang on to that independence is what destroys the new relationship! I'm not saying to foolishly surrender your ability to handle your own business to a man you just met, but you have to know how to be the woman in the relationship just as the man needs to be the man in the relationship.

The saddest type of relationship to witness is one where you have two people together, but they have independent mind-sets within that relationship. For married couples, you see folks that have separate bank accounts, different rules for their own children in the same house, you drive your car and I drive mine—yada yada yada! How in the world can true love exist in that environment? It can't! Love is a sacrifice for the other person, remember?

If this is your mind-set going in, you are already doomed for failure because you have a backup plan in place and your route of escape is already mapped out. Some men may come across as though they want a woman to be totally self-sufficient and independent, but those type of men are selfish and don't want the responsibility of taking care of a woman and a family. If that is his mind-set, he also has a "bailout" plan but may not have told you.

A real man wants to take care of his lady and provide for her and allow her to relax and just worry about being a lady—not out there fixing flat tires, pumping her own gas, opening her own door, and having to pay for everything out her own pocket just because she can.

A real relationship or marriage is about being dependent on the other person, without a backup plan and doing your part to make sure the other person has what they need to succeed in every area of life. I'm sure some of you are thinking, "How can I be sure he has my back?" If you're asking that question, you're probably in the wrong relationship already!

How can you already be in a relationship and not know if someone has your best interest at heart? Why are you still in it, and how did you get into it? Nine times out of ten, you didn't prequalify him or wait long enough before getting involved!

IF THEY CAN DO IT,
WHY CAN'T YOU?

Whenever a woman has learned that her man may frequent strip clubs or has taken interest in another woman, it's almost automatic to ask the question "What does she have that I don't?" The reality is that she really doesn't have any more than you do! The only advantage she may have or ingredient that she uses is her ability to "entice"—that's it!

The whole allure to men going to a strip club is that the women there are unattainable, and they are selling the illusion of being accessible. She is using the same principles described in chapter 1 about not becoming captured and being something that he can't conquer. That is why he is turned on by her: *she is so close, yet so far away*, and that drives a man crazy.

Remember earlier how I said, *"You have to be predictable and unpredictable at the same time, predictable that you will work your female persuasiveness to open his nose up and leave him wanting more, but unpredictable of what reward he will receive"*? Men are a lot like women in the sense that we like surprises too, especially if it involves intimacy!

If you properly set the stage or sell the promise of "the best time of his life" later, by the time you actually touch him or put your hands on him, he's ready to fall over or pass out! Stop going straight to "third base" just because that's what he wants or what he is used to! *Slow seduction in an intimate setting is your trump card!*

Psychologically, men are at the mercy of a woman's ability to seduce and disarm him if he isn't careful. The problem is that everything these days is perverted and used the wrong way. The women (dancers/strippers) that know how to use their feminine persuasion use it for the wrong reasons, such as getting a sugar daddy or to get money from the man without a relationship. It works even though the man knows what she's up to.

She is using the art of seduction and persuasion, which usually the good woman at home doesn't use or has abandoned. That leaves room for an unfulfilled desire in him, but the good news is that God gave every woman that same ability. So *step up your seduction game.*

God made the man to be the physically dominant specimen and He gave the woman the ability to dominate through tenderness and feminine persuasion. Read your Bible; almost every man that dealt with a woman was seduced by her femininity. These men were God's point men, yet the influence of the woman was still able to move that man to do what she wanted him to do.

Look at David and Bathsheba, Samson and Delilah, and, of course, the most monumental example of a woman's ability to persuade—Adam and Eve! Everything that a man craves as far as fame, fortune and material possessions is all in an effort to ultimately get "the woman." Please understand the gift that you have, be confident in it, but use it creatively and wisely because God gave it you!

UNPERFECT TIMING

In this particular section, I'm going to be 1000 percent honest! That's right, *one thousand*! Most men really don't have an issue with doing anything that their woman may ask of them, and from the men I know personally and have interviewed, "unperfect timing" seems to be the reoccurring topic that comes up. Timing timing timing! It's not *what you want, but when you want it* that creates the friction.

I'm sure everyone is familiar with the classic scenario of when a man is watching sports, the woman comes along and wants something done and wants it done right then! Let me give you ladies a glimpse of how a man thinks and processes a scenario like this:

The NBA finals are on, and there are only seven minutes left in the game. His favorite team is trying to make a comeback, and you come in and see that the trash is still overflowing from two days ago. You recall asking him to take it out before the house started to smell, but it's still there. You mention it to him and begin to get upset because he's not responding to you because he is into the game. By this time, your demands become more apparent, you're at the point of being totally pissed off at him, and you tell him you want him to take it out *now*!

A man's way of looking at this scenario is like this: *I know the trash needs to go out, but I need to see if my team is going to win this game. That trash ain't going nowhere and can wait until the game is over. I can't replay the game because it's live and only a few minutes are left.*

In his mind, he is focusing on who wins the game, and the trash being there isn't going to make or break the kitchen or the house! Most women see things in a totally different light. I could be wrong, but from my experience, a woman would be thinking, "Now I know I asked him *two days* ago to take that trash out. Now the house is stinking and he's basically ignoring me while that stupid game is on!"

The key thing to remember here is that "the trash" shouldn't cause an argument and bring division between two people. Both sides will take up their own position and defend it to the point of an argument because he's thinking, "It's not that serious or important that it happens *immediately*," and she is thinking, "I asked him *two days ago*!" How can inanimate objects, like the trash and a game, come between adults?

Ladies, you may not like this next statement, but if the trash is bothering you that much, go ahead and take it out! Why would you set snares for him and allow yourself to get all upset over something so insignificant? Love does for the other person, remember? The house isn't going to catch on fire because the trash doesn't go out in the next ten seconds! Seven minutes left in a game isn't worth two days of arguing or a stand-off with someone you love.

Pride says, "I asked or expect him to do it, so I'm not going to do it," and we all know pride tears things and people apart. So, ladies, it's not the task that you want to have done, but rather the timing. Imagine if he got the urge for some ice cream and demanded of you to get up in the middle of the night and get it for him or while you were in the middle of getting your hair or nails done? Everyone needs their own "moment" in spite of what *we* want them to be doing!

GREAT IS THY UNGRATEFULNESS

Talking to different men and women over the years has really shown me the true nature and differences between the two. Men have a tendency to be less talkative, more bottom line, what's-your-point type of creatures, while women, on the other hand, seem to be more open, talkative, and enjoy going into detail during conversations. Even though men are, or seem to be, rough and rugged emotionally, we are really just as emotional as women. The only difference is the actual *expression of that emotion.* Men tend to express hurt or disappointment through anger, aggression, or by shutting down. Women often express their hurt by crying, consulting a friend, or withdrawing.

A major issue that seems to make its way into men's opinion about dealing with an independent woman or some women is that men often feel underappreciated and taken for granted. When a man isn't admonished, given credit or recognition for any contribution he makes in a relationship or around the house, he will more than likely look for some sort of validation from outside sources. He may start hanging out with the boys, picking up bad habits, or being open to a woman that knows how to say "Thank you." All too often, couples create a routine or define roles and the appreciation for each person's contribution or efforts goes unrecognized.

By overlooking the "thank you" factor, you are leaving a crack or opportunity for another person to come in and make him feel like his efforts matter and before you know it, his attention becomes captured. Something as simple as saying "Thank you" or "Baby, I really appreciate you" goes a long way with a man. You may have a routine where you normally pick up the kids from day care, but on a particular day, he picked them up; it's okay to say thank you even if they are his children.

That would be like you cooking on a regular basis, and after he eats, he just gets up and goes about his business without acknowledging that fact that you cooked or saying "Thank you, that food was delicious." The reality is that no one is required by law to do anything for anyone, so please don't take your partner for granted. Even if you are used to him playing his so-called part or role in the relationship, acknowledgment is essential to letting him know that you see what he does and are appreciative of him being in your life.

You can't base your willingness to do this on if you think he's worthy or not because everyone needs to feel like they matter. Men are, again, very simple to figure out and easy to please; however, pride or past hurts may often stop a woman from giving him what she would easily give to a stranger that may hold a door open for her, the simple human courtesy of saying "Thank you."

I KNOW YOU WANT TO ... BUT ...

It's a very noble and generous position to take from a woman's perspective, but this next issue is regarding a real man's man and how his mind functions. This information may just unlock a mystery that some well-accomplished women might ask themselves from time to time when trying to "bag" a man. I'm going to just put it out there and be honest about it. In the African American community, the black male has had a few hurdles to climb and a gang of social obstacles to overcome, but understand the following dynamic.

Over the past few decades, the African American male has been purposely suppressed and oppressed, which has caused him to, in some cases, fall behind socially and economically. A man facing these circumstances may find himself in a complicated position and may not be aware of how to navigate through it. One thing that doesn't change is the fact that he continues to dream and have aspirations, but the ambition and motivation has dried up. The other thing that's a constant is that he is still a man and has a desire for companionship.

So now we have a man that may not have accomplished a lot on paper or in material possessions but still carries around his primal instincts to have a woman in his life. At this point, he is no different from anyone else; when pressure or discontentment comes, he will default back to any sense of pleasure that he can find, which usually comes in the form of sexual relationships and other unhealthy habits.

Let me set the scene for you: Along comes a woman that may have the missing pieces that this man may lack, and she thinks to herself, "I can help him reach those goals and dreams because I can take some of the pressure off of him." You have a house; he lives in an apartment. You are methodical and pay your bills on time; he seems to be carefree and isn't the best with finances. He tells you his dreams and seems to be a really good man with a good heart, so you both fall into a relationship.

You may have acquired some things over the years or from previous relationships such as tools, yard equipment, etc., things that men generally use. He moves in with you, and you give him access to all that you have to make him feel like you are behind him 100 percent, which is a good thing, by the way.

He seems to be a little uncomfortable with accepting this new life of freedom and support from you, but you can't understand why. As I said earlier, your intentions are noble and commendable; however, this is why your good intentions go bad. A man can't feel comfortable accepting something that a woman has acquired or another man's possessions!

Those two things only remind him that he hasn't attained as much as the next person, especially things such as a house, a particular car, yard equipment, etc., or if there are things that he should have gained on his own at this stage in his life. Call him crazy if you want, but men are designed to earn what they enjoy, and a free ride usually doesn't sit right in his heart if he is truly a good man that wants to take care of his woman.

IF HE SAYS *YES* . . .

By now, you know that I'm trying not to step on any toes, but if I'm going to keep it real, then I have to tell it like it is, so buckle up . . . This topic has almost reached an epidemic level! Women have gotten to a place where they will drop hints, make suggestions, or just outright ask a man to marry her rather than wait on him to propose to her. Please listen up, ladies, if you are at a place where you feel like "He won't ask me" or "I've been waiting forever," then it's not going to happen; and if it does, do you really want it anyway?

Pressuring a man into marriage and him saying yes is like the scenario of someone stealing something for years and not having any remorse, but as soon as they get caught, they all of sudden are sorry for what they did. They aren't truly sorry for their actions, or they would've stopped stealing and returned the merchandise before getting caught! The only reason they are sorry is because they've been exposed and now have a penalty to pay.

So what I'm saying here is that people aren't going to change or really be converted unless they do it on their own, not because they are pressured to! If a man wants to marry you and be seriously committed, it won't come by force or pressure from a woman, children, or any other source other than himself! The men on the other end of this topic may not like this, but here is the truth from a male's perspective: the man that does go ahead and gets married because you continue to ask him is only doing it at this point to shut you up!

A man that has to be coaxed or manipulated into marriage has no intentions on giving up any of his old habits; that's why he didn't want to get married in the first place! He figures that in order to have some peace and to silence your nagging, he might as well do it. You, on the other hand, may be happy initially because he finally married you, but it will definitely be short-lived, and heartbreak is coming.

If soon after the marriage you begin to argue or trip because he's hanging out again, hiding his phone, acting sneaky, etc., his thoughts may sound something like this: "Oh well, you're the one that wanted to get married" or "you knew I wasn't ready so you get what you get." It's unfortunate, but people don't change because someone else wants them to—they change because they want to.

If a man really wants to be married to you, what's stopping him from asking you? "Will you marry me?" are words that are spoken, and if he's not deaf and can talk, then what's really stopping him? If you get excuses, like "Baby, I just want to wait until I get my money right" or "I'm working on my career first, and it's for us," you could be wasting your time. If a man knows that you are the one for him, there is no way he's going to let you get away or take a chance of losing you.

Proverbs 18:22 says that "*he* who finds a wife, finds a *good* thing." So my question to you is, are you a good thing? If so, why are you asking him? He should be looking for and asking you!

MIRROR . . . MIRROR . . . ON THE WALL

Every morning when you get out of bed and go into the restroom, you may at first, walk right past the mirror. Sometime before leaving the house, you make your way back to that mirror. Of course, you want to make sure that your hair is combed, your teeth don't have food in them, your clothes are looking okay, and that your overall appearance is up to par.

Mmmm . . . I wonder why you feel all of that would be necessary before facing the world every day. Could it be that the mirror gives you an assessment of how you appear? The truth of the matter is that if you did see something out of place, you would be quick to correct it so that you could be at your best, right? *Thank God for mirrors* because the reflection gives us a chance to fix some issues that might otherwise be overlooked and embarrassing.

It's amazing how we take care of our bodies and outward appearance automatically and without thought, but when it comes to guarding our inner spirit man, we just allow ourselves to get beat-up, mistreated, and abused. Why is that? Maybe it's because we don't look into our invisible mirror that gives us a reflection of the condition of our souls.

Many women and people in general don't know what that invisible mirror is, but wouldn't it be nice to have one in the natural so we could fix our emotions like we do our appearance? Women spend countless hours in front of a mirror, primping and prepping to make sure every hair is in place, the eyeliner is straight, and the lipstick is on point. But let me ask a question: how much time daily are you looking into your soul?

If your soul is out of place or a little crooked, what do you do to adjust it? If you are disappointed with yourself because of poor decisions you continue to make, how do you fix it? If you're unhappy with the way your life is going, what cream can you use to turn it around?

The issues discussed in this book can't be fixed by applying more makeup, upgrading your weave, getting a pedicure, shopping till you drop, adding to your shoe collection, or anything else women do to make themselves feel better. Unfortunately, we can't look into a physical mirror to see the problems brewing in our souls, nor can we apply natural remedies to spiritual issues. There is however a way to see your heart and soul where all of these issues reside; you have to look into your supernatural mirror, the Bible.

If your Honda broke down, you wouldn't take it to a Chevy dealership, would you? Why then when your life and emotions are turbulent or you heart is broken would you listen to TV, radio, or friends who didn't take part in creating you? In order to get fixed, you've got to go back to the original manufacturer—God! He designed and created you, so He is the only one that can help you through every scenario you may face in this life. Every area that you are weak in is where He is supposed to come alive if you let Him!

The Bible says "in our weakness, His strength is made perfect." So if you have areas of your life that you lose control or continue to fall short in, that's when you have to allow Him to carry you and do it for you. We aren't designed to handle everything that comes our way, but He is, so there's no need to fear. Look at it this way: the things you can control, control them . . . the things you can't control, you can't. So either way, why worry?

ARE YOU A DO-IT-YOURSELFER?

I'm quite sure you've heard the phrase "God bless the child that has his own," but that doesn't mean that you do everything on your own. Most people start to think that they are more than they really are after acquiring some sense of accomplishment or when they have reached a certain social status. An independent woman, or a "do-it-yourselfer," thinks that she can "do it on her own." But I've got news for you—you can't!

If in fact you could do everything on your own, answer the following questions: Why didn't you grow the food you eat? Why didn't you manufacture the car you drive? Why didn't you build the house you live in? Do you get my point? Everyone has to depend on someone else for something, and that goes for men and women alike. We are made to depend on God for the things we have need of, but we also can't leave each other out.

Women that take the position that they don't *need* men are missing out on a blessing that God put in place to enhance their lives. A car doesn't *need* oil in it to run, nor do the tires *need* air to roll, but it's only a matter of time before a breakdown happens. Life is so much better when lived out in balance and the way it was designed to be lived. Everything in this life has to have a balance that's designed by God.

Medicine when taken correctly can heal you; you take too much, it can kill you. A car is designed to take you places; when misused, it can become a deadly speed trap. Water is necessary for all living things, but if you ingest too much, it will drown you. So as you can see, all things must be done in moderation, properly handled and used according to God's original intent, including relationships.

As we established earlier, anyone can be independent, but we weren't created to be. If a woman had absolutely no *need* of a man, how then would children come into the world? How would mankind evolve? Or how would generations continue if every woman wanted to be this new-age Ms. Independent? You may not have a desire to be in a relationship with a man, but that's more than likely due to hurt or past relationships that devastated you.

Your body is even designed for a man, and a man's body is designed for yours; if it were not so, we would all have the same body parts. That's why two men being together cannot produce children nor can two women. Whether you admit it or not, God made the two different genders for a reason, and He has a kingdom purpose for doing so.

Do you *need* a man? No, I'm not saying that you do; but a car doesn't *need* oil and air in the tires either, remember? Will a car run smoother and function better after adding those things to it? Absolutely! The same goes for a healthy relationship; life can go a lot smoother if you get in the relationship that God is in control of, not one you picked yourself.

I'm certainly not advising you to go out and get a man because you are physically designed to complement each other, but what I am saying is that you can't allow past hurts and bad experiences to govern how you view the next man because he could be your blessing! Please just make sure you consume the nuggets of wisdom in the previous chapters and apply them before going all in. And remember let the man find you because you are a *good thing*!

Written by

Ronny E. Myles

Inspired by

God

NOTES

Printed in the United States
By Bookmasters